THE GIFTS OF THE SPIRIT

**A Bible Study of the Gifts of the Spirit
For
Children, Teens and Adults**

By
David Walters

**Illustrated, Graphic Designs, and Layout
by
Jessica Ellis Age 15**

Published by
GOOD NEWS FELLOWSHIP MINISTRIES
220 Sleepy Creek Rd.
Macon, GA 31210
Phone: 478-757-8071 Fax: 478-757-0136
e-mail: goodnews@reynoldscable.net
web site: goodnews.netministries.org

International Standard Book Number: 978-1-888081-68-6

Many thanks to everyone who helped me produce this book, especially Jessica Ellis who did the illustrations and much of the graphics, and my patient secretary, Sharon Busby. Together we spent many hours fine-tuning and learning how to cope with the program. The manuscript was written about seven years ago, so it was like a movie, "Seven Years in the making." Satan hindered us many times, but praise the Lord, we finally succeeded. I have taken liberty in not working too hard to make this book grammatically correct. The reason being, that if I did, I felt it would make the book somewhat boring and complicated for the children. I wanted them to feel I was speaking directly to them. I hope that I have succeeded. I trust that home school parents and teachers, will not be too upset with any bad grammar which they may find.
David Walters

Chapter One
Holy Spirit Baptism

Children! Before I teach you about the gifts of the spirit, I need to explain about being baptized with the Holy Spirit. Being a Christian is more than just having Christ in your heart. It is being filled with the Holy Spirit which is God's power and anointing. Why do we need power? To defeat the devil, to live a godly life, to have victory over sin and temptation and to be bold when we preach and pray for other kids to be saved.

You don't just automatically get baptized with the Holy Spirit as soon as you believe. You have to be ready for the Holy Spirit to have His way and fill up your life with Himself.

Try to imagine an empty glass. Then fill it up to the top with nice fresh clean water. That's good to drink, especially if you are dry and thirsty. Now! if the glass was half filled with dirty crud: like smelly muddy water with dead bugs in it and your mother topped it up with nice clean water, you wouldn't drink it. Right? You would want her first to empty out the crud, wash the glass out real good and then fill it up with nice clean water.

So be ready to surrender to the Holy Spirit, confess any sin or rebellion in your life and ask the Lord to fill you up. A suggested prayer could be something like this:-

Lord!
I need you power. I need to be set free from fear and shyness. I need to be victorious and bold as a Christian. I confess and repent from every sin and fear which hinders my walk with you. I surrender myself to the power of your Holy Spirit. Please fill me now with the Holy Spirit. I receive your Holy Spirit by faith and believe You are filling me right now.
Amen!

At this point wait on the Lord, Take a deep breath and breathe in the Holy Spirit like you would air, and then expect to feel the His presence and power filling you. Don't be in a hurry. Wait as long as necessary and just keep believing and receiving. Remember! God really wants to fill you with His power. He certainly doesn't want kids to be spiritual wimps. Also remember His promise:

"If you then being evil, (sinners) know how to give good gifts to your children, how much more will your heavenly Father give the Holy Spirit to those that ask Him " (Luke 11:13).

As you are being filled with the Holy Spirit, you might feel hot, or kind of weak in the knees. Or you might even feel real sorry for your sins, or your friend's sins, and become weepy or shaky. You might also feel happy. You might even feel like shouting and perhaps a funny language could feel like bubbling up in your mouth, and you find your-selves speaking in other tongues. So! Don't worry, just enjoy God's love, power and presence.

Now that you have been baptized or filled with the Holy Spirit, its time to learn about the gifts.

Question Time

1. Why do we need the baptism of the Holy Spirit?
   (circle the correct answer)

A. To be popular.   B. To have power. C. To be cool. D. To please our parents.

2. Why do we need power?
   (Fill in the blanks)

A. To defeat the _____
B. To live a _____ life.
C. To have _____ over sin and temptation.
D. To be _____when we preach and pray.

3. When do we get baptized with the Holy Spirit?

(Circle the correct answer)

A. When we become adults.   C. When our parents give us permission.
B. As soon as we believe.   D. As soon as we are ready for the
                                    Holy Spirit to have His way.

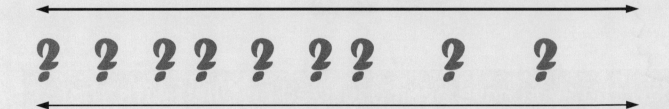

Chapter Two **The Gifts of the Spirit**

What are the gifts of the spirit? A lot of kids aren't taught about them, so they either don't understand, or they don't even know about them. This book is written to show and tell you about them and also how you as a kid can have these gifts and use them in your work for the Lord.

Remember that when we become Christians, it's more than just believing in Jesus and learning how to be good. God has a lot of things for us to do. The Christians in the Bible did all kinds of things, like preaching the gospel, healing the sick, casting out demons, prophesying, and working miracles.

How would you like to do those kind of things? Some kids get bored just sitting around waiting for Jesus to come back, but God has a job for us to do before Jesus returns and the gifts of the spirit are like tools that are given to us to use. You see tools are used to make or repair things. So the gifts of the spirit are given to us Christians so we can make people better, if they are sick, lost, or in trouble.

Spiritual Gifts

1 Corinthians 12:1,4-11

1   Now concerning spiritual gifts, brethren, I do not want you to be ignorant:

4   There are diversities (different kinds) of gifts, but the same Spirit.

5   There are differences of ministries, but the same Lord.

6   And there are diversities of activities, (different functions) but it is the same God who works all in all.

7   But the manifestation of the Spirit is given to each one for the profit of all:

8   For to one is given the word of wisdom through the Spirit, to another the word of knowledge through the same Spirit,

9   To another faith by the same Spirit, to another gifts of healings by the same Spirit,

10 To another the working of miracles, to another prophecy, to another discerning of spirits, to another different kinds of tongues, to another the interpretation of tongues.

11 But one and the same Spirit works all these things, distributing to each one individually as He wills.

(NKJ)

These are the scriptures that we will be learning about. You may not quite understand what the verses mean, so I will try to explain them to you in the **next chapter.**

Question Time

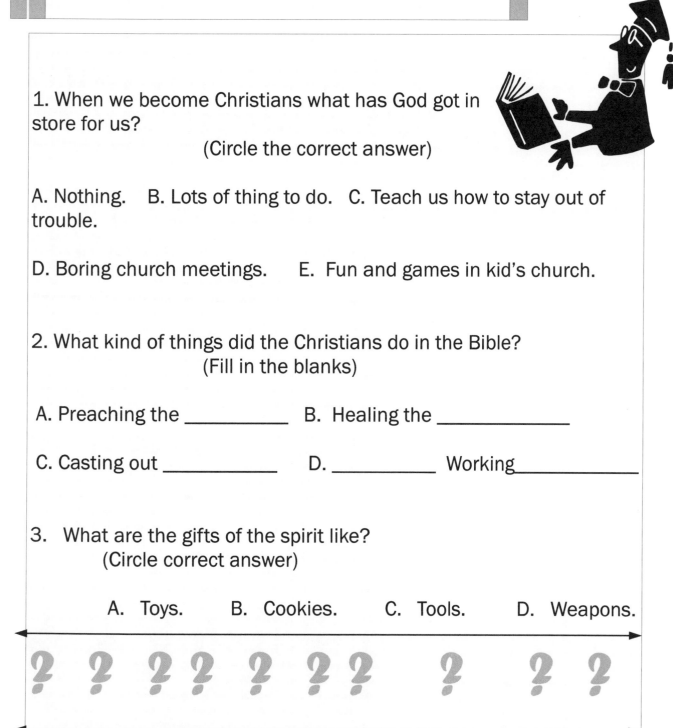

1. When we become Christians what has God got in store for us?

(Circle the correct answer)

A. Nothing.   B. Lots of thing to do.   C. Teach us how to stay out of trouble.

D. Boring church meetings.   E. Fun and games in kid's church.

2. What kind of things did the Christians do in the Bible?
(Fill in the blanks)

 A. Preaching the _____   B. Healing the _____

C. Casting out _____   D. _____ Working_____

3. What are the gifts of the spirit like?
(Circle correct answer)

A. Toys.   B. Cookies.   C. Tools.   D. Weapons.

Chapter Three

Explaining the Gifts

First of all, in verse one the Apostle Paul, (who wrote 1.Cor.12) says he doesn't want us to be ignorant about spiritual gifts. That means he does not want us to be dumb when it comes to understanding about spiritual gifts. Kids are not suppose to be dumb about the important things which God has for us. So Paul wrote to try to explain what they are, what they do, and how they work.

In verse 4. He says there is only one Holy Spirit, but there are different kinds of gifts.

Actually there are **nine** gifts listed. **That's quite a lot isn't it?**

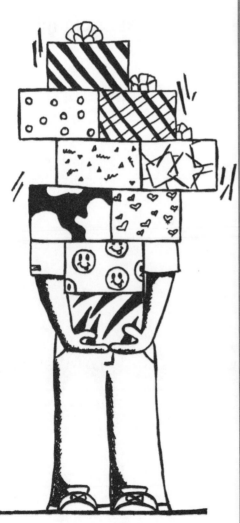

Verse 5. There are different ways of serving God. Pastoring, Evangelizing Prophesying, Teaching, and starting new churches (which is what Apostles do), but the same Lord.

Verse 6. There are different ways in which the gifts are used.

Verse 7. A gift is given to each person to benefit everyone. In other words God gives you a gift not to keep, but to give away to bless others. If you do that then He will give you another gift to give away. For example, if somebody is sick, God may give you the gift of healing to pray for them to be healed. If someone needs a special word of encouragement or direction, He may give you a prophesy or a word of knowledge or a word of wisdom for that person.

Children don't know a lot and they don't usually have a lot of wisdom, but God has all knowledge and wisdom, so He can give kids a word of wisdom or knowledge to give to others.

Verse 8-10 These are the different kinds of gifts that are listed. There are nine of them. Some Bible teachers have divided them into sets of three. The first three are **speaking** or **verbal** gifts. They are Prophesy, Speaking in Tongues, and Interpretation of Tongues. These three enable us (make us able to) **talk** like God.

The second three are **thinking** or **internal** gifts. They are the Word of Wisdom, the Word of Knowledge, and the Discerning of Spirits. These three enable us (make us able) to **think** like God.

The last three **power** or **action** gifts. They are Faith, Miracles and Healing. These three enable us (make us able) to **act** like God. Isn't that awesome? Imagine Christian kids going around speaking, thinking, and acting like God, instead of just goofing around and being silly all the time.

Verse 11   The Holy Spirit has these gifts divided and given out to individual people as He sees fit.

Question Time

1. What does ignorant mean?
   (Circle correct answer)

A. Old.   B. Young.   C. Dumb.   D. Clever.   E. Popular.   F. Ugly.

2. How many gifts are there?
   (Circle correct answer)

A. 9   B. 1000   C. 642.   D. Zero

3. The gifts are given to enable us to _____ _____ _____ like God.

(fill in the blanks)

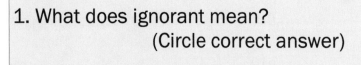

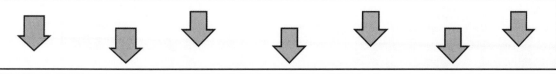

Chapter Four The Nine Different Gifts

Let us now look at these different gifts:

Prophecy

What is prophecy? There are two kinds of prophecy. One is telling about what is going to happen in the future. The Old Testament prophets often prophesied about things which the Lord had told them were going to happen. Sometimes it was warnings God that was giving to His people, if they did not straighten up and stop sinning. Sometimes the bad things that were going to happen, didn't happen or were delayed, because the people repented and began to serve God again. Also some prophesies were promises of the good things that God was going to do in the future, because He loves His people.

The prophesies we want to look at are words given by God for individuals for **edification, exhortation and comfort.** (See 1 Cor. 14:3). (I will explain what those three words mean later.) True prophecy is God speaking through a human mouth. God wants to tell us things and He uses Christians who are sensitive and yielded to Him. Although there are people called to be prophets you don't have to be an official prophet to prophesy. Kids and teenagers can prophesy if they are open and surrendered to God. It's one of the gifts of the Spirit. I've seen many kids prophesy when the anointing of the Holy Spirit has come upon them. As we focus on God and ask Him to use us to bless others, you may sooner or later, begin to feel you have a message. You may not have the whole message, only part of it; but if you obey the Holy Spirit and go to the person and start to prophesy the whole message will usually come.

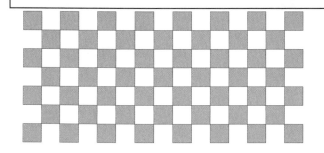

You go over to the person and say, "I believe the Lord has given me a prophecy for you, would you like to hear it?" If they say yes, then go ahead and prophesy. Remember! God will not give you a prophecy that is against what He says in the Bible, so if you are not sure, check with your pastor or parents before you give out the prophecy.

When I first learned about prophecy, I was too scared at first to do it in a church meeting. I thought I might dry up and forget what the Lord was telling me. I also thought that the Pastor or the elders might tell me to sit down and shut up, because I was wrong and my prophecy wasn't from God.

So I went home and I practiced on myself. How? When I was at home I went to my bedroom and I began to prophesy to myself, believing that God was speaking to me - through me. It was so awesome, that I very soon became bold in giving out prophesies when God told me to.

When I prophesied to myself, the Holy Spirit told me that I was anointed and that God was going to use me to preach to many people and He would use me mightily. I believed it and started getting bold and confident. Remember, prophecy is for edification, exhortation and comfort. Edification means to build up

PROPHECY IS FOR EDIFICATION, EXHORTATION AND COMFORT.

people or encourage them. Exhortation means to inspire them to do great things for God. Comfort means to help people when they are having a hard time by letting them know that God has not forgotten them and He really cares.

So if we really love the Lord and want to minister like **Jesus** did, then we will not be selfish; but we will be eager to prophesy, so that we can bless and serve others.

Question Time

Prophecy

1. What is true prophecy?
   (Circle correct answer)

A. Saying good things are happening.   B.   God speaking through a human mouth.   C.   Saying bad things are happening.
   D. Saying what we like.

2. What do you have to be or do to prophesy?
          (Circle correct answer)

A.   Be an official prophet.   B. Attend a school of the prophets
C.   Be sensitive and yielded to the Holy Spirit.
D.   Be an experienced Christian.

Speaking in other tongues

Speaking in other tongues is very much like prophecy. It is the Holy Spirit speaking out of you, but this time he is using a heavenly language. This is a hard gift to understand. When we were babies, we gurgled and spoke gibberish or baby talk, and we don't like the idea of doing that again, especially now that we know how to talk properly. But try to understand this, most kids when they pray, soon run out of things to say. Why? That's because they only have little minds. They don't usually think a lot and they are only interested in what happens in their life. Their world is small. It's Dad, Mom, family, school, friends, and play, and that's about it. Kids don't usually know what's happening all over the world. They are not normally interested in the government, politics, wars, and disasters. So they don't usually pray about those things.

When you have the gift of tongues you can pray about those things even though you don't understand much about them.

When you pray in tongues, you are praying with the spirit, not with your understanding. And when you pray in English, or your native tongue, you are praying with your understanding and not with your spirit. When you sing in the spirit, you are singing in tongues and not with the understanding. When you sing with the understanding you are singing in English, or your native tongue, not with your spirit."

"**What is the conclusion then? I will pray with the spirit, and I will also pray with the understanding. I will sing with the spirit, and I will also sing with the understanding**" (1 Corinthians 14:15).

Once you have that gift, you can pray or sing about everything. Awesome! Also the devil gets mad, because he doesn't under- stand what you are saying How come? Because the Bible says you are speaking mysteries to God. Satan doesn't understand mysteries. "He that speaks in an unknown tongue speaks mysteries to God."

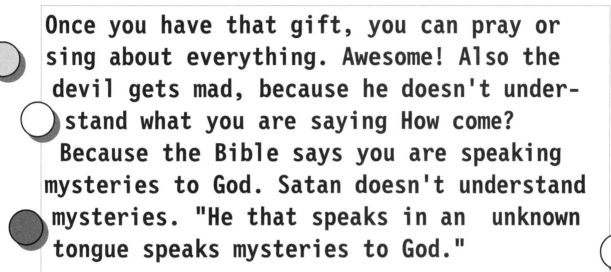

"He that speaks in an unknown tongue speaks myster- ies to God."

For he who speaks in a tongue does not speak to men but to God, for no one understands him; however, in the spirit, he speaks myster- ies" (1 Cor. 14:2).

Interpretation

Also at church you can give out a message in tongues, and someone should be able to give the interpretation. What's interpretation? As the Lord moves on you, a message in tongues is coming up from your spirit, you open your mouth in faith and shout it out. It may be short, or quite long. It doesn't matter, you just have to obey God and do it. Then people wait for an interpretation and the Holy Spirit moves on someone else, who gives out your message in English. This enables everyone to understand what God is saying.

Remember, to receive this gift, you must cooperate with the Holy Spirit. Open your mouth, move your lips and tongue, and make a sound. Don't try to think up words in your head and don't start speaking or praying in English or your native tongue. Just fix your mind on Jesus and let those words come out. "But I don't understand what I am saying! I haven't learned how to do it!" You don't do it by learning. There are no schools that teach tongue talking courses. Just do it! And don't listen to the devil, who will tell you it's stupid and you are making it up. Use your faith, surrender your will and mind to God, give Him your voice and tongue, and out those heavenly words will come.

Once you have received this gift, you can pray every night in tongues before you go to sleep. The more you do it, the easier it will become, and the stronger prayer warrior you will be. From time to time the Lord will use you to give out a message in tongues in church or children's church. That will be exciting, so don't forget to be obedient and do as the Lord says.

Speaking in Other Tongues

What is speaking in other tongues?
(Circle correct answer)

A. Talking gibberish. B. Speaking French.
C. Speaking Spanish.
D. Speaking a heavenly language.   E. Speaking about the Bible.

2. How do we speak with tongues?
(Circle correct answer)

A. Surrender our voice and tongue to the Holy Spirit.
B. Take a tongue talking course.
C. Keep practicing.   D. Copy people who know how to do it.

3. Why should we pray in other tongues?
(Circle correct answer)

A. Because it's fun.   B. Because it's stupid. C. To exercise our mouth.
D. To pray the will of God, when we don't understand.

4. Why should we speak in other tongues?
(Circle correct answer)

A. So people will think we are crazy.   B. To give out a message from God.
C. To show off. D. To set people free. E. To show little kids how to do it.

? ? ?? ? ? ? ?? ? ? ? ?

Interpretation of Tongues

Interpretation is different than translation. The Bible has been translated. It was originally written in the Greek and Hebrew language. Clever people, who understood those languages, copied them into English, so you and I could understand what the Bible says. They didn't just sort of tell you what it meant, but they studied every word and found out what each word meant in the English, then wrote it down. That's called a translation. When our daughter Lisa was a little toddler, we couldn't understand what she said when she spoke, because she talked baby talk. Faith, her sister, who was three years older than her, told my wife and I what Lisa was saying. Faith was Lisa's interpreter.

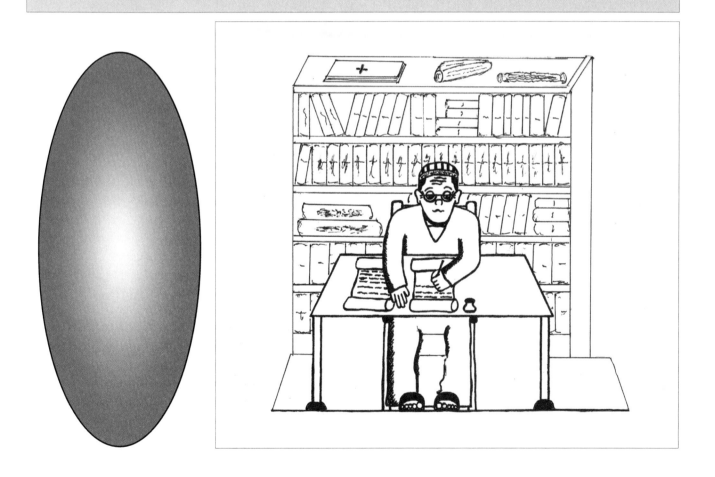

When you hear someone giving a message in tongues, you won't understand the language they are saying, but sometimes you will feel like the Lord is telling you what it means; or you may feel a strong desire to speak out a message in English. That's probably God giving you the gift of interpretation. He wants you to open your mouth in faith and speak it out to bless the congregation. "What happens if I mess up?" you might say. As you learn, you will make mistakes, but that's alright. It's better to try and make a mistake, than to never try at all. God doesn't rebuke (scold) us for trying and messing up, but He does rebuke us for never trying; especially if it's because we are afraid to make a mistake or become embarrassed.

The gift of interpretation is not given to you as a special gift to keep and use anytime you want. If that was so, then you would become the official church interpreter. Many years ago that is what some churches did. The pastor's or deacon's wife would give the message in tongues and the pastor or the deacon would give the interpretation. No one else ever got a chance. But the gifts are given to everyone at different times to use as the Holy Spirit seems fit. In one meeting, you may get the gift to use and another time God may give it to someone else to use.

Question Time

Interpretation of tongues

1. What does interpretation mean?
   (Circle correct answer)

A. Figuring out things.   B. Explaining the meaning.
C. Giving out an idea.   D. Copying one language into another.

2. How do you interpret?
   (Circle correct answer)

A. Sharing what you believe God is explaining to you.
B. Keeping quiet.
C. Reading the Bible.
D. Quoting the Bible.

Chapter Five The Next three gifts

Word of Wisdom

We know that God is all wise, so all wisdom comes from Him. People aren't always wise and don't always behave wisely. Kids and teens are usually less wise than the adults. Older people are supposed to become wise as their hair turns grey. But even the oldest and wisest person in the world doesn't compare to God. Even King Solomon who was known for his great wisdom, made mistakes and messed up. God's wisdom is awesome, He can't mess up or make a mistake. Sometimes Christians need special wisdom to give to people who are in trouble and need advice or help. That is where the word of wisdom comes in.

Your mom or dad could be having a problem that you don't understand. You would not know what to tell them; but God may give you a word of wisdom for them that will be just what they needed to hear. Jesus was a filled with wisdom when he was only twelve years old.

"And the Child grew and became strong in spirit, filled with wisdom; and the grace of God was upon Him"   (Luke 2:40).

IF CHRIST LIVES IN YOU THEN HIS WISDOM CAN BE GIVEN TO YOU AND YOU CAN SPEAK OUT THAT ANOINTED WORD THAT HE HAS PUT IN YOUR HEART. IF YOU, OR YOUR FAMILY, OR YOUR FRIENDS, ARE GOING THROUGH A PROBLEM THAT YOU DON'T HAVE AN ANSWER FOR, ASK GOD FOR A WORD OF WISDOM AND SEE WHAT HE WILL DO.

There is a true story of a bunch of kids who were on their way to a prayer meeting at a house (during a time in history when it was against the law to have religious meetings, except in official church buildings.) The kids were stopped by soldiers, who were looking for Christians that were having illegal secret prayer meetings. The soldiers asked the kids where they were going? The older kid, (a girl of about eleven) spoke up. She couldn't tell them that they were going to a prayer meeting, as they would all be arrested and thrown in jail. She also couldn't lie, as she was a Christian, so she asked the Lord for a word of wisdom. This is what the Lord told her to say. "Our older brother has died and we are going to find out what he has left us in His will" The solders let them go on their way. You see their elder brother was Jesus and he had died for their sins. They wanted to find out more about all the blessings of heaven, the gift of eternal life, and the gifts of the Holy Spirit, that He has left for them.

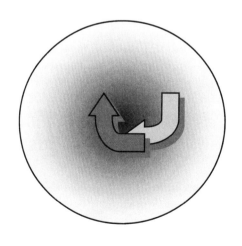

Question Time

Word of wisdom

1.) Who can get a word of wisdom?
(Circle correct answer)

A. Wise people. B. Preachers only. C. Anybody. D. Kids only.

2.) If kids are usually foolish, how can they act wise?
(Circle correct answer)

A. Getting the best education. B. Becoming street wise.
C. Being a "wise guy" or a "smart Alec." D. Receiving God's wisdom.

3. What did the little girl say to the redcoat soldiers?
(Fill in the blanks)

Our older brother has _____ and we are going to find out what he has_____ us in his _____

Word of Knowledge

The Word of knowledge is similar to the word of wisdom. As God is all wise, He is also all knowing. He knows every-thing. You can hide things from people, you can even hide things from your parents; but you can't hide things from God. He knows all about us. I have often thought that if everything that we have ever said, thought and done, was put on an overhead at church on Sunday morning for everybody to see, most us would not want to show up at church. We would either be too ashamed or embarrassed. Aren't you glad that God shows us mercy and doesn't condemn us, because we are not perfect?

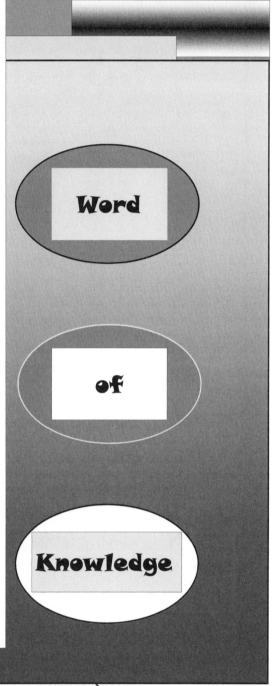

We don't know everything. There are lots of things we are ignorant about. The younger you are the less you know. Most kids know far less than what adults know. God is not going to show us everything. The Bible says that

> The secret things belong to the Lord our God, but those thing which are revealed belong to us and to our children forever..."
> (Deut. 29:29)

The word of knowledge is a spiritual gift from God given to us as we minister to people. Sometimes you may be praying for someone and you receive a word of knowledge about them, that you couldn't possible know. I remember praying for a man once and the Lord told me he had lost his job and the Lord was going to give him a better one. After I prayed for the man, he told me that he lost his job the day before. Another time a little boy asked me to pray for his dad, who wasn't saved and he had left him and his mom. The Lord told me to tell the boy that the man would be saved and return to his wife within six weeks. Some months later, I met the man and his wife in a meeting and they told me it happened just like I said.

God can use kids to do things like that. Jesus did it with the women at the well when He told her she had had five husbands and the man that she was now living with wasn't her husband.
(see John 4:7-19)

Peter used the word of knowledge when he told Ananias and Sapphira that they had lied against the Holy Spirit. (see Acts 5:3) The word of knowledge is a very powerful gift to get people's attention. One Sunday morning, a young evangelist in our church in England, got up and said, "There are five people here in the sin of immorality, and if you all don't stand up and confess and repent I will stand in front of you until you do." All those people stood up and confessed their sins and most of them were first time visitors.

A word of knowledge is a very powerful gift to get people's attention!

Well how do kids get words of knowledge? The same as anyone else. Don't make the mistake of thinking that because your a kid, you don't qualify. If you believe that God is your Heavenly Father and Jesus is your shepherd, then expect to hear His voice. (see John 10:3-4)

When you learn these lessons on the gifts
have a time of practicing them on each other.

In my "Children's Prayer Manual," I teach on how to
hear God's voice. As we pray and fellowship with
our Lord we must expect Him to lead us by His
Spirit and tell us what to do and what to say. This is
especially important when we are learning to
minister. It's a waste of time teaching children about
the gifts of the Spirit, if the kids never have an
opportunity to try them out. Practice make perfect.
Perhaps your church will hold a "School of the Spirit"
for the kids. When you learn these lessons on the
gifts, have a time of practicing them on each other.
Ten or more kids can be taught together in a class
and then practice prophecy, the word of wisdom,
or the word of knowledge on each other. Pray for
one another and ask God if He will give you a word
for your partner. You'll be surprised how obliging
God can be.

One little girl of about seven, was filled with the Holy Spirit in one of my meetings. The next day she went to the shopping Mall with her Grandma. While she was there, the Lord began to give her words of knowledge for some of the people at the Mall. She said to her Grandma, "We must pray for that lady, because her husband has just died and she is feeling very sad and lonely." Then the little girl saw someone else and said, "This man has lost his job and we need to pray for him to get another job soon." Her Grandma was amazed at her little granddaughter, who had all these words of knowledge about these people. The Lord can use you in the same way with the word of knowledge.

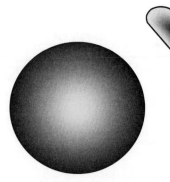

Question Time

Word of Knowledge

1.) How can you get a word of knowledge?
   (Circle correct answer)

A. Listen to God.   B. Read lots of books.
C. Read encyclopedias. D. Practice for quiz programs.

2.) Why does God give us a word of knowledge?
     (Circle correct answer)

A. So we can look cool in front of others.   B. So we can know everything.
C. To help other people.   D. So people can rely on us.

3. What do we do if God gives us a word of knowledge?
    (Circle correct answer)

A. Keep it to ourselves. B. Ask God who it's for and then give it to them.
C. Give it to anyone and everyone.

4. When should you give a word of knowledge.
    (Circle correct answer)

A. Anytime.   B. When the Lord gives you the O.K.
C. When your parents give you permission. D. Over the telephone in secret.

? ? ?? ? ? ?? ?

Discerning of Spirits

The word discernment means to be able to know the fake from the real. This usually come with experience. Everybody has been tricked by someone, sometime or other. Most people have been taken in by a liar, or a con-man. When people experience this kind of thing, they soon learn how to be cautious and not believe everything that people tell them. They also learn how not to trust everybody. Some liars and con artists are so good at what they do, that they can deceive people over and over again.

Kids are usually born with trusting hearts, so they easily trust others. That's why parents tell their children not to speak to strangers. The problem is that people who kidnap kids don't usually look like strangers. They are usually so nice and friendly that the kids get taken in and go off with them. Kids could also easily trade something valuable for something cheap, because the thing offered to them looks expensive. This a well known true saying, "all that glitters is not gold."

The gift of discerning spirits is not some-thing that comes with age and experience. It is a gift from God. You can't fool God, so if God gives you that gift you can't be fooled either. The discerning of spirits is given for certain situations. This means when there is a need to figure out what's true and what's false, God can give you that gift for that moment. Discerning of spirits really means this. How to know the difference between the Holy Spirit, an evil spirit and the human spirit.

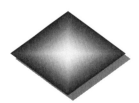

Sometimes kids have temper tantrums. We know that is not the Holy Spirit, but is it an evil spirit that is making the kid do that, or is the kid just being rebellious? If it's an evil spirit, then no matter how many times you tell the kid to behave, it probably won't work. You have to cast the evil spirit out first. On the other hand if the kid always throws a fit every time he can't have his own way, then its probably due to lack of discipline from his parents. No amount of prayer or trying to cast evil spirits out of him will work. The best thing for him is probably a good spanking and training him to obey and respect his parents or teachers.

Sometimes people go to a church meeting and if they see something happen that they don't understand, they get scared and think it's the devil. That may or may not be true. Other people can go to a church where strange things happen and make the mistake of thinking it's all of God. Other people go to a dead old church where it's boring and nothing ever happens, and they think it's of God. That's why we need the gift of discerning of spirits. Evil spirits can also be religious and tell you that all the miracles, signs and wonders, were finished when the Bible was written. Those religious spirits will tell people that we don't need those things today and that people or churches that believe and practice those things are controlled by the devil. Then some people who don't know any better and don't really believe the Bible, but only believe what their denomination teaches them, can fall into the same trap.

This might seem very confusing to kids, that's why we need that gift. God can speak to our spirit and give us peace when we don't always understand with our minds. There is going to be a number of times when you have to decide whether the thing that is happening or being said, is from God, the devil, or people. In other words does it originate (begin or start) with God, the devil, or human nature. Of course if it goes against the teaching of the Bible, then we don't have to accept it.

Question Time

Discerning of spirits

1.) What is discerning of Spirits?
    (Circle the correct answer)

A. Knowing the difference between evil spirits, the Holy Spirit, and the human spirit. B. Knowing the difference between the good, the bad, and the ugly. C. Choosing cool friends. D. Only hanging out with people that you know.

2.) How do you operate in this gift?
    (Circle correct answer)

A. Being old and mature. B. Being street wise.
   C .Listening to the Holy Spirit.   D. Listening to older kids.

3.) How do you become accurate in using this gift?
    (Circle correct answer)

A. Practice.   B. Use it at Christmas and Easter only.
   C. Use it on little kids only. D. Wait until you are an adult.

The Last Three Gifts
Faith

We have all been given faith. Nobody does or goes anywhere without exercising faith. When you go to bed you believe that your bed won't collapse. You believe that the walls won't fall out and the ceiling will not drop on you in your room. When your dad or mom drive the car, they believe it will work. When they drive on the Interstate, they don't stop at the top of a hill and look over just to make sure the road is still there. You may have never been to Australia, but you believe it exists. As I have said before, everybody has faith.

Christians believe all those things mentioned, but they also believe in God, in Jesus, and in the Bible. "The gift of faith," which we are now discussing, is more than the faith I just mentioned. It's a special gift from God, given to us at special times for special needs. Let me give you an example. Imagine your grandpa is very sick and everyone thinks he is going to die. You start to pray for God to heal him, and if you are given the gift of faith, you suddenly sense this great peace coming upon you, and now you know grandpa is going to be O.K. Even though others are still worried, you are not, because you really know that God has healed him. You have received the gift of faith. Sometime later the phone rings and you hear that granddad is better. You just knew it would happen.

Another way this gift works is this. People are being prayed for in your church. Some people need to be healed or need some kind of miracle. You start to pray for them, asking God to heal them or give them a miracle. Suddenly, as you are praying, you feel this confidence and assurance come on you and you become bold. Then you say something like this:

"Receive your healing in the name of Jesus!"

"In the name of Jesus be healed, or receive your miracle in Jesus name" and you know the gift of healing is coming to them. You walk away feeling confident, even though you may not see them healed right away, you know it's going to happen.

Question Time

Faith

1.) What is the gift of Faith?
   (Circle correct answer)

A. Believing in Jesus and the Bible.
B. Knowing you prayer has been answered.
C. Believing that your bed won't collapse, or the ceiling won't fall down on you.

2.) How does the gift of faith work?
   (Circle correct answer)

A. It gives you assurance that what you believe will come to pass.
B. It makes you doubt.
C. It kind of makes you hope.
D. It makes you confused.

3.) What happens when you use the gift of faith?
      (Circle correct answer)

A. You become scared.   B. You become bold. C. You become cool.
D. You become stupid.   E. You become weird.

The last three gifts

Healing
The gift of healing is like the gift of faith, you know when you have it. You can pray for people to be healed, and trust and believe that God will heal them, but the gift of healing is different. This is when you have been given the power to heal someone. You can feel the Lord's healing anointing on you and His power to heal is flowing out of your hands. As you touch the sick person and say, "Be healed in Jesus Name," the gift of healing is passed on to them and they are healed.

Remember the story of Peter and John when they met the lame man outside the temple who was begging for money? What did Peter say to him? "Look to God?" or "I will pray for God to bless you?" or "I will invite you to our church where our pastor can pray for you?" or "Next week we are holding a healing meeting?" or "Here's a few dollars?" No! What Peter said was, "Look on us, we don't have any money, but what we do have we give to you. In the name of Jesus Christ of Nazareth rise up and walk." Peter had the gift of healing for the man who was lame. (See Acts 3:6)

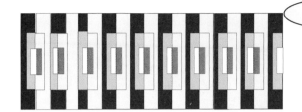

If God gives you the gift of healing, it's not for you to keep and then tell everybody that you have the gift of healing. No! It's to pass on to that sick person, so that God can heal them. In other words, the gift is not for us, (unless we are sick) but to give away to those who need a touch from God.

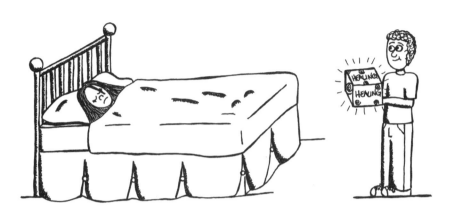

The gift of healing is available to us, so we can do what Jesus did. "And Jesus went about Galilee, teaching in their synagogues, preaching the gospel of the kingdom, and healing all kinds of sickness and all kinds of disease among the people" (Matt. 4:23).

Question Time

Healing

1.) Who is the gift of healing for?
  (Circle correct answer)

A. For the sick person.
B. For me to keep.
C. To trick people.

2.) What happens when you receive the gift of healing?
        (Circle correct answer)

A. Ask someone to pray for the sick person.
B. You take them to a healing meeting.
C. You give them the gift of healing.
D. You take them to the doctor.
E. You take them to a worship meeting.

3.) What happens if they don't get healed right away.
        (Circle correct answer)

A. You give up.   B. You tell them it's not God's will for them to be healed.
C. You tell them they don't have enough faith.   D. You keep on believing.

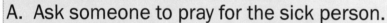

Working of Miracles

Working of Miracles and healing often go together, but miracles are greater. Jesus did lots of miracles. He turned water into wine, multiplied the loaves and fishes, calmed the storm, walked on water and raised the dead. Then there are miracles like opening blind eyes and deaf ears. Twisted limbs suddenly start growing straight. People who couldn't walk, suddenly leap out of their wheel chairs and start running. These are acts that are impossible. In other words, they are things that can't normally happen. It's God's supernatural power touching our lives.

M I R A C L E S

Not only were these done in the Bible days, but throughout history these things have also happened. Men and women of God have performed miracles many times. In my special meetings people have seen miracles happen when children have prayed for them. In one of my meetings, a little 8 year old girl named Zoe, prayed for a man who had been in a wheel chair for 6 years and he jumped out and began to walk.

Over the years I have held miracle services and I have asked the children to pray for the adults. If the anointing has been on them, God has used them. Several people who were blind in one eye began to see, after the children prayed for them, and many deaf people began to hear as well. People in pain for years were instantly healed. So healings and miracles often go together, and all this happens, because God grants to us that special gift of faith, healing and miracles. What wonderful gifts God has for us to use for His glory.

EVEN TODAY SOME PEOPLE ARE BEING RAISED FROM THE DEAD. CANCERS AND TUMORS HAVE DROPPED OFF OF PEOPLE'S BODIES AND THERE HAS EVEN BEEN REPORTS OF NEW BODY PARTS GROWING BACK. LIKE A LEG, OR ARM, OR FINGER, OR HAND, THAT HAD BEEN CUT OFF IN AN ACCIDENT. WE NEED TO BELIEVE TO SEE AND PERFORM MORE MIRACLES TODAY, BEFORE JESUS RETURNS.

Every miracle doesn't have to be big, but it can still be a miracle. I remember, when my wife Kathie, had invited a pastor and his wife over to our house for supper. She made spaghetti and it was just about ready to serve when she realized that she had forgot to make any meat sauce. She said, "Oh Lord what shall I do? I don't have time to make any now, and I don't have any meat. Please help me!" Just as she prayed, the door-bell rang. When I opened the door, one of our church members was standing there. He said, "My wife felt the Lord tell her to make you this and have me bring it over to you." Guess what! It was a big dish of meat sauce to go with the spaghetti. You see God will perform miracles, even with the simplest of things, if you believe.

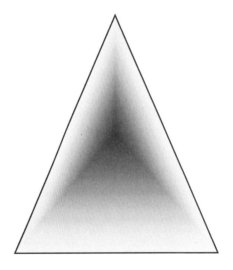

Question Time

Working of miracles

1.) What are miracles?
   (Circle correct answer)

A. Impossible acts   B. Making people feel better.
C. Being kind. D. Taking vitamins or medicine.

2.)   Name four miracles that Jesus did.

A._____
B._____

C. _____
D._____

3.) Circle the correct answer

A. Miracles are only found in the Bible.   B. Miracles are for today.
C. Miracles are not for today. D. Only the devil performs miracles.

Chapter Seven

Dealing with Difficulties

Some people have different opinions about spiritual gifts. I believe that all of the gifts are available for everyone who wants them. There are people who don't believe in the gifts at all. They think they were only for Bible days. They are wrong of course. Then other people believe that the gifts (especially tongues) were not given to everybody, but just to certain people. They quote what the apostle Paul said,

"Do all have gifts of healings? Do all speak with tongues? Do all interpret?" (1 Corinthians 12:30).

It sounds as though he expects us to say No!, but not really. You see, Paul also says, "I wish that you all spoke with tongues. . . . " (1 Corinthians 14:5)

So what is he talking about? Well! He is saying that the gift of tongues can be used anytime for private praying, but not everybody needs to be giving out messages in tongues in church. If that happened it might cause a lot of confusion. He says that two or three messages is quite enough and they should be followed with the gift of interpretation.

"If anyone speaks in a tongue, let there be two or at the most three, each in turn, and let one interpret" (1 Corinthians 14:27).

Some people say the only thing that we have to concentrate on is love. The quote the following scriptures. "Love never fails. But whether there are prophecies, they will fail; whether there are tongues, they will cease; whether there is knowledge, it will vanish away. For we know in part and we prophesy in part. But when that which is perfect has come, then that which is in part will be done away" (1 Corinthians 13:8-10).

They say the perfect is the Bible. We now have the Bible, so we don't need those gifts anymore. But they don't want to say, we don't need knowledge anymore. You see that scripture also says that knowledge will vanish away. The perfect that Paul is talking about, is not the Bible. He is talking about when Jesus returns to the earth, and sets up His kingdom. Jesus is the perfect one. God has given us all the gifts to be used right up to the end of time. Isn't that exciting?

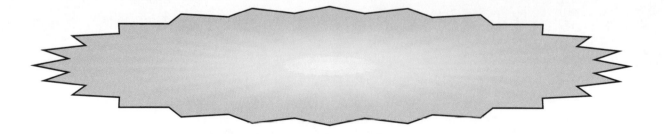

Question Time

1.) Who are the gifts for?
   (Circle correct answer)

A. For everyone.
B. For no one.
C. For preachers only.
D. For special people only.
E. For everyone who wants them.
F. For people who don't want them.

2) What does "perfect has come" mean in 1 Corinthians 13:8-10?
   (Circle correct answer)

A. The Bible. B. The greatest Christian.
C. The return of Jesus or the second coming of Christ.
D. A new church building.

3. How many people should give a message in tongues in a church meeting?
   (Circle correct answer)

A. 100.   B. The whole congregation. C. 2 or 3.   D. As many as want to.
E. None.

4. How many people can pray in tongues?
   (Circle correct answer)

A. 3. B. As many as want to. C. 72   D. Only elders and deacons. E. No one.

Chapter Eight
Exercising Spiritual Gifts

If you don't exercise you will not become strong and develop good muscles. If all of us just lay in bed, or sat in a chair all of our lives, we would become so weak that we wouldn't be able to walk, run, or jump. Very old people find it hard to walk, because their muscles have shrunk and don't function like they should. Sometimes it's because they stop exercising. There are places for old people to go and exercise. The doctors say that old people should keep exercising, because it will keep them young and active.

A baby moves a lot. After a few months, it kicks it's legs and waves it's arms in the air. It's exercising it's muscles. When a little child learns to crawl and walk, they say that it moves so much, that if grown ups did the same as the toddler, they would be worn out in a couple of hours.

Kids run a lot, it's hard to get them to just walk. They use a lot of energy in running around, climbing, jumping and playing. They don't always realize it, but they are developing their muscles by exercising.

What about the need to exercise spiritual gifts? If we don't, our spiritual muscles will shrivel up and we will become spiritual wimps. Remember many of those gifts can be used in many places and not just in church. Your school, the shopping Mall, the playground, the park, the beach, McDonalds, a friend's house and even in your bedroom. I'm sure that you can think of other places where you might practice or exercise your spiritual gifts.

I mentioned this before, if your church is open to this, then a "School of the Spirit" would be a good thing for kids to join. There you can learn, practice and even make mistakes. Remember the saying, "Practice makes perfect" and "If at first you don't succeed, try, try, again." Some kids may try once or twice and if it doesn't work right away, they quit. Let's not be like that. Let's not be quitters or losers. Let's be winners. Let's be willing to keep on try-ing, keep on exercising, keep on pushing through and obey the Lord. He does want to use us, so we must be willing to take the time and learn.

Question Time

1.) How do you become good at using spiritual gifts?

(Circle correct answer)

A. Thinking about them.   B. Not thinking about them.
C. Hearing about them.   D. Using or exercising them.
E. Praying about them.   F. Watching others do them.

2.) When are the gifts to be used?
(Circle correct answer)

A. Only in church. B. Anywhere. C. Only in bed.
D. Only in a church meeting.   E. Only at McDonalds.

3.) How often should we exercise spiritual gifts?
(Circle correct answer)

A. Tuesdays and Sundays.   B. When on vacation.
C. Every God given opportunity. D. Never.
E. When the other kids do.   F. When our parents say its ok.

Chapter One

Question 1.= B

Question 2. Correct Blanks A = Devil
B = Godly C = Victory D = Bold

Question 3 = D

Chapter Two

Question 1 = B

Question 2 Correct Blanks
A = Gospel   B = Sick   C = Demons
D = Prophesying   E = Miracles

Question 3 = C

Chapter Three

Question 1 = C

Question 2 = A

Question 3
Correct Blanks = Talk. Think. Act.

Chapter Four

Prophecy

Question 1 = B

Question 2 = C

Speaking in other Tongues

Question 1 = D

Question 2 = A

Question 3 = D

Question 4 = B

Interpretation of Tongues

Question 1 = B

Question 2 = A

Chapter Five

Word of Wisdom

Question 1 = C

Question 2 = D

Question 3
Correct Blanks = Died. Left. Will.

Word of Knowledge

Question 1 = A

Question 2 = C

Question 3 = B

Question 4 = B

ANSWERS TO ALL THE QUESTIONS
DO NOT CHEAT! REMEMBER, CHEATING IS A SIN. DO NOT CHEAT!

59

Discerning of Spirits

Question 1 = A

Question 2 = C

Question 3 = A

Chapter Six

Faith

Question 1 = B

Question 2 = A

Question 3 = B

Healing

Question 1 = A

Question 2 = C

Question 3 = D

Working of Miracles

Question 1 = A

Question 2 Fill in Blanks = Turned water into wine. Multiplied Loaves and fishes. Calmed the storm. Walked on water. Raised the dead. (Choosing any four of the five lists is acceptable)

Question 3 = B

Chapter Seven

Question 1 = E

Question 2 = C

Question 3 = C

Question 4 = B

Chapter Eight

Question 1 = D

Question 2 = B

Question 3 = C

60

A Spiritual
Encounter"
Reaching the Children
and Youth of the
World

TWO CHOICES.
Raising A Generation Of Anointed Children And Youth
or
Equipping The Younger Saints

SPECIAL FAMILY WEEKEND
PLUS A ONE DAY TRAINING SEMINAR

Equipping Youth Pastors, Sunday School Teachers, Children's Workers, Nursery Workers, Parents, Children, and Teens.

The opportunity is available to your church to sponsor one of these dynamic seminars. Author and speaker David Walters has been imparting a fresh vision and anointing to parents and those that work with children and youth.

◆ Teenagers do not have a junior Holy Spirit and children don't have a baby Holy Spirit!
◆ Children are not filled with the Holy Spirit for entertainment, or a couple of object lessons!
◆ The average church-wise child and teen can be turned around and set on fire for God!
◆ Christian teenagers do not have to surrender to peer pressure - they can become peers!
◆ Strong willed children and rebellious teenagers can become loving and obedient.

David Walters has written a number of books including, **Kids in Combat, Children Aflame, The Anointing and You, Equipping the Younger Saints, Radical Living in a Godless Society and 6 Children's Illustrated Bible Study books**. His articles have also appeared in many publications including Charisma and Ministries Today.

"David Walters is initiating the most awesome will of God for any specialized ministry." **- Paul Cain**

"David Walters is doing for youngsters what we are doing for adults." **- Dr. Bill Hamon**

"David Walters introduces children and youth to the power of the Holy Spirit and then trains them." **- Bob Weiner**

"David Walters is anointed to lead even the very young into moving with the gifts of the Holy Spirit" **- Roberts Liardon**

To schedule a weekend or for more information

1- (800)300-9630

**GOOD NEWS FELLOWSHIP MINISTRIES
220 Sleepy Creek Rd.
Macon, GA 31210
Phone: 478-757-8071 Fax: 478-757-0136
e-mail:goodnews@reynoldscable.net
web site:goodnews.netministries.org**

Mighty Young Warriors Conference With David & Kathie Walters

CALLING ALL MIGHTY YOUNG WARRIORS!!

EXCITING ANOINTED WORKSHOPS

Prophesy -that means telling people what God is saying

Intercession - pray the heart of God, not wimpy prayers

Evangelism -how to tell your friends about Jesus

Miracles -how to pray for the sick and see them healed.

Good News Ministries
220 Sleepy Creek Rd.
Macon, GA 31210
1(800)300-9630

PARENTS WILL NOT BE LEFT OUT!

SPECIAL MEETING WITH KATHIE WALTERS!

Did you know that the supernatural realm is meant to be a normal part of your life? The angels, the heavenly visitations are for you AND your family. If this is part of your own life it will also be part of your child's life. Come and get rid of the religious mindsets that keep you out. This is meant to be a non-religious Spirit time for big kids like you & me.

Other Titles by David Walters

Kids in Combat. Training children and youth to be powerful for God.
(For parents, teachers and youth pastors)

Equipping the Younger Saints. Raising Godly children and teaching them spiritual gifts.
(For parents, teachers and youth pastors)

Children Aflame. Amazing Accounts of children from the journals of the great Methodist preacher John Wesley in the 1700's and David's own accounts with children and youth today.

The Anointing & You/Understanding Revival. What must be done to Receive, Sustain, Bring , Impart, and to Channel the Anointing for Renewal/Revival, and to pass it on to the Younger Generation.

Worship fur Dummies - David Walters calls himself a dummy in the area of praise and worship, but he knows the ways of the Holy Spirit.

Radical Living in a Godless Society - Our hedonistic secular society really targets our children and youth. How do we cope with this situation?

Other Children's Bible Studies by David Walters

Armor of God - Illustrated children's Bible study of Ephesians 6: 10 - 18. (For children ages 6-15 years)

Being a Christian - Illustrated children's Scripture study on being a Christian (For children ages 6-15 years)

Children's Prayer Manual - Children's Illustrated study on prayer (ages 6-14 years)

Fact or Fantasy? - Illustrated children's study in Christian apologetics. (For children ages 9- 17 years)

The Fruit of the Spirit - Illustrated children's Bible study on bearing fruit. (For children ages 7-15 years)

Books by Kathie Walters

Angels - Watching over You - Did you know that Angels are very active in our everyday lives?

Bright & Shining Revival—Account of the 1948-52, outpouring of the power of God on the Hebrides Islands, Scotland.

Elitism and the False Shepherding Spirit — Control, manipulation, Spirit of abortion, grief and it's devastating results.

Health Related Mindsets - Explanation of mindsets which can bring sickness.

Celtic Flames – Exciting account of famous 4th & 5th Century Celtic Christians: Patrick, Brendan, Cuthbert, Brigid and others.

Columba - The Celtic Dove - Read about the prophetic and miraculous ministry of this famous Celtic Christian, filled with supernatural visitations.

Living in the Supernatural - Kathie believes that the supernatural realm, the Angels, miracles, and signs and wonders are the spiritual inheritance of every believer, as in the early church. She tells how to embrace and enter our inheritance.

The Visitation - An account of two visitations from the Lord that Kathie experienced. One lasted for seven days and the other for 3 1/2 weeks. Also a visitation her daughter, Faith had when she was just 17 years old.

Parenting - by the Spirit - The author shows how she raised her children by listening to the Holy Spirit rather than her emotions.

The Spirit of False Judgment – Dealing with Heresy Hunters. Sometimes things are different then what we perceive them to be.

Seers List – An explanation of the Prophetic Seer anointing. Depicting Biblical instances of the Seer ministry and how it operates today.